A NEW DEAL FOR WOMEN: THE EXPANDING ROLES OF WOMEN 1938–1960

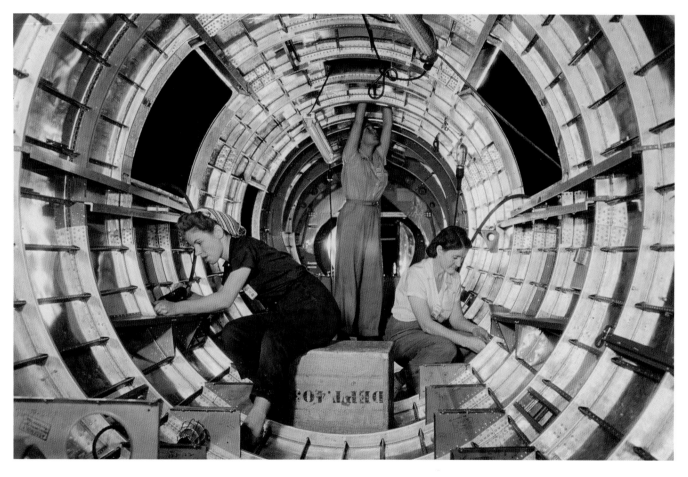

PATIENCE COSTER

CHELSEA HOUSE
An Infobase Learning Company

A NEW DEAL FOR WOMEN: THE EXPANDING ROLES OF WOMEN 1938–1960

Library of Congress Cataloging-in-Publication Data

Coster, Patience.
  A new deal for women : the expanding roles of women, 1938–1960 / Patience Coster.
     p. cm. — (A cultural history of women in America)
  Includes index.
  ISBN 978-1-60413-934-1
  1. Women—United States—Social conditions—20th century—Juvenile literature. 2. Women—United States—Economic conditions—20th century—Juvenile literature. 3. Feminism—United States—History—20th century—Juvenile literature. 4. United States——Social conditions—1933–1945—Juvenile literature. 5. United States—Social conditions—1945—Juvenile literature. I. Title. II. Series.

  HQ1420.C66 2011
  305.40973'0904—dc22
                    2010045959

Project management by Patience Coster
Text design by Jane Hawkins
Picture research by Shelley Noronha
Printed and bound in Malaysia
Bound book date: April 2011

10 9 8 7 6 5 4 3 2 1

This book is printed on acid-free paper.

The publishers would like to thank the following for permission to reproduce their pictures:
akg-images: 7, 10, 15; The Art Archive: 31 (The Library of Congress); Corbis: 5 (B. Anthony Stewart/National Geographic Society), 6, 8 (Bettmann), 9 (Bettmann), 11, 12 (Bettmann), 13 (Genevieve Naylor), 17 (Bettmann), 19 (Bettmann), 20 (Bettmann), 25 (CinemaPhoto), 26 (H. Armstrong Roberts/ClassicStock), 27 (Hulton-Deutsch Collection), 30 (O. Johnson/ClassicStock), 32 (Bettmann), 34 (Robert Sisson/National Geographic Society), 35 (Schenectady Museum; Hall of Electrical History Foundation), 37 (Bettmann),40 (Jim Mahoney/Dallas Morning News), 42 (Michael Ochs Archives), 43 (Justin Locke/National Geographic Society), 46 (Bettmann), 49 (Underwood & Underwood), 51, 55 (Bettmann), 56 (Condé Nast Archive), 58, 59 (Bettmann); Getty Images: 14, 16, 18, 24, 28 (Time & Life Pictures), 29 (National Geographic), 41 (Time & Life Pictures), 45 (Time & Life Pictures), 47 (Alfred Eisenstaedt/Time & Life Pictures); The Kobal Collection: 23 (Paramount), 33 (AMC), 38 (Universal), 44 (Columbia), 48 (20th Century Fox), 57 (20th Century Fox); B. Matthews: 21 (Collection of the Museum of Mississippi History, Mississippi Department of Archives and History); Rex Features: 39 (The Everett Collection), 53 (The Everett Collection); Social and Public Art Resource Center (SPARC): 54; TopFoto: 22 (The Granger Collection), 36, 50 (Keystone Archives/HIP), 52 (The Granger Collection).

Contents

THE PERIOD OF HISTORY COVERED BY THIS book—World War II and its aftermath—had a dramatic impact on women's lives. By the 1920s, many women had already cast off their modest, 19th-century ways by abandoning restrictive clothing, behavior, and attitudes in favor of shorter skirts and independent, unconventional activities outside the home. The introduction of voting rights for women injected their lives with new confidence. But this decade of easy money and reckless consumer spending was brought sharply to a halt in 1929, when the American stock market collapsed.

During the 1930s, years of austerity and economic depression brought many women back into the home to support their husbands in their search for work. However, in poorer families, where male long-term unemployment was commonplace, women had to earn money working outside the home to make ends meet. By 1938, North America was emerging from the Great Depression, but three years later it was plunged into war. World War II propelled women into a new and wider sphere of activity. As men went overseas to fight, there was a huge increase in the number of women taking on men's jobs.

During the 1950s, female independence was limited since the men had returned from war to reclaim their jobs. Women were actively promoted as homemakers, serving and supporting their husbands and children. Home and the family came to symbolize a safe refuge from the horrors of the Cold War and possible nuclear attack. However, while the lives of many women seemed limited by convention, the activities of others—for example, those at the forefront of the civil rights movement—would help bring about radical change.

Left: In 1952, a first lieutenant and his bride walk under an arch of swords at the U.S. Military Academy, West Point, New York. For many young women in the 1950s, a white wedding was a dream come true.

66

A WOMAN'S VIEWPOINT

"There should be more of us directing [movies]. Try as any man may, he will never be able to get the woman's viewpoint in directing certain stories. . . . A great percent of our audience is women. That too is something to think about."

Dorothy Arzner, movie director (*Dance, Girl, Dance*), interviewed in the 1930s

5

CHAPTER I

NEW ERA, NEW WOMEN

To understand the situation in which women found themselves in 1938, it is necessary to look back a decade and a half to a significant moment in the history of female suffrage. By 1920, American women had won the vote. This battle produced a generation of steely campaigners who were determined to achieve female equality in education and the workplace.

TURNING POINT

HOUSEWIVES' LEAGUE

The Housewives' League of Detroit was founded on June 10, 1930, by Fannie B. Peck to address problems of poverty among black families. The league protested against stores and businesses that charged high prices for essential goods and services. It also lobbied businesses to hire black employees. Soon other similar housewives' leagues sprang up across the United States.

VOTING RIGHTS

On August 26, 1920, a constitutional amendment was adopted giving women voting rights throughout the United States. The fact that women could now influence the outcome of elections meant that politicians at last had to listen to their concerns. Nevertheless, women still found it hard getting their voices heard in traditionally male-dominated sectors such as politics, business, and industry. A particular area of female interest was that of social welfare. During the 1920s, women such as Eleanor Roosevelt lobbied government on issues including child labor and emergency relief programs. But it was only when her husband, Franklin Delano Roosevelt, became president in 1932 that her ideas began to be put into practice.

RELIEF PROGRAMS

Franklin D. Roosevelt came to power at the height of the Great Depression. He introduced a package of reforms, known as the New Deal, to address the country's economic problems. Government agencies, such as the Works Progress Administration (WPA) and the National Recovery Administration (NRA), were created to

Left: Eleanor Roosevelt (at right) was a passionate campaigner for social justice and women's suffrage. This photo, taken in the early 1930s, shows Roosevelt and fellow activist Nancy Cook putting up a poster in New York City to advertise the National Recovery Administration.

Above: The Works Progress Administration funded cultural projects, for example, in theater, fine art, and music. Here a women's trio, employed by the WPA, sings for radio stations WSBT and WFAM.

help provide new jobs for the unemployed. Influenced by his wife, Roosevelt encouraged female participation in politics, appointing women to professional positions in various New Deal programs. By the end of 1933, thirty-five women had been appointed to prominent government posts. By the end of the 1930s, fifty-five women held key positions in government.

THE NEW DEAL

Women were employed at various levels in New Deal programs. At the time, most trained social workers were women. But the WPA only hired single women and widows because federal policies discouraged married women from getting jobs. In any case, most married women were unable to take on full-time work because they were almost entirely responsible for the domestic duties of home and family; the New Deal did nothing to help with the absence of day-care facilities for young children, for example. Therefore, most female WPA workers did relatively menial work,

> **BREAKTHROUGH BIOGRAPHY**

FRANCES PERKINS (1882–1965)

Frances Perkins was born in Boston, Massachusetts. She was interested in the problems of working people, especially the working poor, and in 1910 became head of the National Consumer's League (NCL), where she lobbied for better working hours and improved working conditions. In 1929, Governor Franklin D. Roosevelt promoted Perkins to the post of Industrial Commissioner of New York, the chief position in the state's Department of Labor. In 1933, as president, Roosevelt appointed her Secretary of Labor, making her the first woman in the United States to hold a cabinet post. It was largely thanks to Perkins's influence that Congress passed the Fair Labor Standards Act.

TURNING POINT

THE FAIR LABOR STANDARDS ACT

In 1938, the Fair Labor Standards Act (Wages and Hours Act) established a minimum wage of 25 cents per hour and a maximum working week of forty-four hours. This ruling applied both to men and women. The act also prohibited labor by children under age sixteen. It resulted in an increase of wages for one in every four workers in the sewing trades.

Below: A maid cleans the staircase in a Washington home. In the 1930s, 70 percent of working black women had jobs as low-paid domestic servants in private houses.

such as laboring in sewing rooms or producing clothing for the poor. Others taught in nursery schools and adult education, repaired and cataloged library books, served hot lunches to schoolchildren, canned produce for distribution, and worked as helpers to older and disabled people.

UNION MEMBERSHIP

Despite the opposition of the Supreme Court, Roosevelt introduced minimum-wage laws in seven states in the early 1930s. This improved the situation of the lowest-paid women workers. The New Deal also supported laws protecting the rights of labor unions to organize. This meant that poorly paid workers could gather to lobby for their rights and protest against exploitation. The number of women joining labor unions skyrocketed: by 1938 more than 800,000 women belonged to unions, three times the number in 1928. However, the unions were not evenhanded in their treatment, and sanctioned lower wages for women than men.

WOMEN IN THE WORKPLACE

In the 1920s and 1930s, most middle-class working women were employed as teachers, nurses, secretaries, typists, file clerks, and salesgirls. Their working-class contemporaries, including black and immigrant women, worked in the textile industry, took in boarders, or did domestic jobs for long hours and low pay. Nevertheless, the numbers of female professionals increased, with some women becoming editors and pharmacologists and occupying important positions in banks and department stores. However, very few women swelled the well-paid ranks of male-dominated professions such as law, medicine, engineering, and architecture.

The economic slump had the unexpected effect of creating more equality for some poorer women. Poverty and male unemployment caused parents to abandon traditional gender roles. More women went out to work so that their families could survive. However, working women were often viewed with suspicion, accused of taking jobs away from men who needed them more. There was even a belief that women working "unnecessarily" for "pin money" had caused the Great Depression and weakened the moral fiber of the nation.

EDUCATION

Despite the increase in females enrolling at college in the 1920s, the younger generation seemed little interested in achieving equal treatment for women. The old-style suffragists of the early decades of the century seemed dull and frumpy to young women who had grown up in the shadow of World War I. As a reaction, these younger women wanted more fun and less seriousness in their lives. Also, while male and female students were encouraged to compete with one another academically, girls were brought up to think of themselves ultimately as wives and mothers, not career women.

In general, opportunities for women were fewer during the 1930s. Some states introduced laws against hiring women because work was so scarce during the Great Depression. Female college graduates were encouraged to take up voluntary work rather than accept a salary. Married women were expected to stay at home and care for their families, and most wives accepted this as their lot. However, despite the emphasis on family, the birthrate dropped because more couples used contraceptives. By 1940, nearly every state had legalized the distribution of birth-control information.

REJECTING FEMINISM

"Feminism has become a term of opprobrium [scorn] [for the young]. . . . The word suggests either the old school . . . who wore flat heels and had very little feminine charm, or the current species who antagonize [annoy] men with their constant clamor about maiden names."

Journalist Dorothy Dunbar Bromley, writing in 1927, predicts a generation of women with little interest in the fight for female equality.

Below: During the 1930s, an increasing number of working women joined labor unions. These members of the International Ladies' Garment Workers' Union, photographed in Chicago in February 1935, are striking for higher wages for workers in cotton goods factories and shops.

CHAPTER 2

WOMEN IN WORLD WAR II

WOMEN'S LIVES CHANGED DRAMATICALLY AS A RESULT OF WORLD War II. In 1941, when the United States joined the war on the side of the Allies against Germany, Japan, and Italy, millions of American men went off to fight overseas. Their departure shook up the notion of what was appropriate work for women. Workers were desperately needed to keep the country going and to support the war effort, and American women were asked to help.

Above: Women install fixtures on board a B-17 bomber at Douglas Aircraft Company, Long Beach, California, in 1942. The starting pay for women working in an aircraft plant was much higher than that offered to female workers in a regular factory.

THE HOME FRONT

Between 1940 and 1945, six million women went to work for the first time. Fewer men in the workforce meant that women were employed to do traditionally male jobs in manufacturing and industry. The huge increase in working women was bolstered by those who were married and middle aged, reflecting a shift in public attitude. Working was now considered part of being a good citizen, and a working wife was doing her patriotic duty—so long as the arrangement was seen as temporary and did not constitute a sexual revolution that would threaten the structure of family life.

ROSIE THE RIVETER

To dispel any doubts that women might have about their new role, political and social leaders swung the media into action with a brilliant propaganda campaign. "Rosie the Riveter" was launched as the iconic image of the female factory worker, the girl who gamely took on tough masculine tasks, armed with nothing more than a spotted bandana, a pair of overalls, and a determined manner. Captivating illustrations by J. Howard Miller

WOMEN'S WORK

"*Women are more patient, industrious, painstaking, and efficient about doing the same thing over and over again. They do the monotonous, repetitive work . . . that drives a man nuts.*"

National Metal Trades Association, "Women in Industry," Chicago, 1943

Left: The mass media praised the millions of new female workers who joined the labor force during World War II. The image of Rosie the Riveter as a national heroine was used to encourage women to take on "men's jobs" and to do them well.

ALL-AMERICAN GIRL

"*While other girls attend their fav'rite cocktail bar
Sipping Martinis, munching caviar
There's a girl who's really putting them to shame
Rosie is her name
All the day long whether rain or shine
She's a part of the assembly line
She's making history, working for victory
Rosie the Riveter*

"*Keeps a sharp lookout for sabotage
Sitting up there on the fuselage
That little frail can do more than a male will do
Rosie the Riveter*"

"Rosie the Riveter," lyrics by Redd Evans and John Jacob Loeb, 1942

OVETA CULP HOBBY (1905–95)

Oveta Culp Hobby was a businesswoman and politician. She became the first director of the Women's Auxiliary Army Corps, helping Edith Nourse Rogers to push the bill authorizing women's participation in the U.S. Army through Congress. She achieved the rank of colonel and received the Distinguished Service Medal for her efforts during the war. She was the first woman in the army to receive this award. Following the war, in 1953, she was appointed as the first Secretary of Health, Education, and Welfare.

("We Can Do It!") and Norman Rockwell in the *Saturday Evening Post* strengthened her appeal. Suddenly assembly-line work was made to seem glamorous: working-class women, who could earn far higher wages as real-life Rosies than in domestic jobs, flooded into aircraft factories and munitions plants. With their help, industrial production doubled between 1939 and 1945.

Women took over jobs maintaining the railroads and trains that carried supplies and troops. They also worked in factories making uniforms and parachutes and as telephone operators and in the electronics industry, where they were believed to have nimbler fingers and a greater tolerance for repetitive tasks than men. They were nevertheless still excluded from top positions at work, for example in the professions such as law and medicine, deciding policy (including policy on running the war), and managing business.

WOMEN IN THE MILITARY

Military leaders quickly realized that women could perform a vital role as members of the armed services. They launched recruitment drives, including rallies, national advertising campaigns, community outreach programs, and appeals to college students.

NURSE CORPS

More than 59,000 nurses served in the U.S. Army Nurse Corps during World War II. They were deployed in the United States and throughout the world wherever American soldiers were stationed. Nurses served overseas in combat zones, under fire in field hospitals, on hospital trains and ships, and as flight nurses on medical transport planes. The work was exhausting

Left: In March 1945, a U.S. Navy flight nurse attends a badly wounded marine on the airstrip on the island of Iwo Jima. The urgent need for female recruits during World War II meant that military service was opened to women on a mass basis for the first time.

Left: A Women's Auxiliary Army Corps recruit repairs the axle of an army truck. Although they did heavy work, women were barred from many aspects of warfare. The military was segregated not only by sex but also by race: just 6 percent of WAAC personnel were African American.

and the living conditions were challenging, but the experience broadened their lives, together with their expectations regarding job prospects after the war.

THE ARMED FORCES

In 1941, Congresswoman Edith Nourse Rogers met with General George C. Marshall, the army's chief of staff, and told him she intended to introduce a bill to establish an army women's corps, separate and distinct from the existing Army Nurse Corps. The Women's Auxiliary Army Corps (WAAC) was established to work with the army "for the purpose of making available to the national defense the knowledge, skill, and special training of the women of the nation." The army would provide WAACs with food, uniforms, living quarters, pay, and medical care. However, women officers would not be allowed to command men; they were to serve in an "auxiliary" capacity only.

About 150,000 women served in the WAAC during World War II. As increasing numbers of men were sent overseas, women replaced them in the workplace. At first, servicewomen took over administrative and clerical jobs to "free a man to fight." But before long, women were serving in almost every occupation except direct combat.

WOMEN OF COURAGE AND CONVICTION

**THÉRÈSE BONNEY
(c. 1912–72)**

Thérèse Bonney was a photographer best known for her pictures taken during World War II on the front between Russia and Finland. Her images of homeless children and adults, the innocent victims of war, touched millions of people in the United States and abroad. She believed the conflict threatened the very existence of civilization and described her heroic journeys into the war-torn European countryside as "truth raids." "I go forth alone," she said, "try to get the truth and then bring it back and try to make others face it and do something about it." She was twice decorated for military bravery.

WOMAN OF THE MOMENT

"The war in general has given women new status, new recognition. . . . Yet it is essential that women avoid arrogance and retain their femininity in the face of their own new status. . . . In her new independence she must not lose her humanness as a woman. She may be the woman of the moment, but she must watch her moments."

From a pamphlet titled "Boy Meets Girl in Wartime," published in 1943 by the American Social Hygiene Association

Among other things, they worked as mechanics, electricians, gunnery instructors, flight instructors, radio operators, stock controllers, cryptologists, and photograph and map analysts. They served worldwide, in North Africa, the Mediterranean, Europe, the South Pacific, China, India, Burma, and the Middle East.

WAVES

On July 31, 1942, Congress approved legislation that allowed for the creation of Women Accepted for Volunteer Emergency Service (WAVES), a division of the U.S. Navy that consisted entirely of women. This authorized women for military duties beyond the medical field in emergency situations. The word "emergency" implied that the participation of women was temporary, as a result of a crisis situation, and would end once the war was over.

A significant difference between WAVES and WAAC was that the latter was an auxiliary organization, serving alongside the army. In contrast, WAVES was an official part of the navy and its members had the same rank and pay as men. This meant the navy was prepared to accept not just a large number of enlisted women, as it had during World War I, but female commissioned officers to supervise them.

Under the command of Mildred McAfee, the first female commissioned officer in U.S. naval history, women served in traditional roles, such as clerical workers and record keepers, and in less traditional ones, such as airplane mechanics, radio operators, medics, and, in communications, intelligence, science, and technology. Within a year, 27,000 women had enlisted for WAVES, and over 85,000 served during the course of World War II.

Left: A poster encourages women to join the WAVES. In 1942, Eleanor Roosevelt had convinced Congress to allow a women's wing of the navy. By the end of its first year, the WAVES was 27,000 strong.

Left: WASPs Frances Green, Margaret Kirchner, and Ann Waldner leave their plane *Pistol Packin' Mama* in a break from training at Lockbourne Air Force Base. Female pilots were restricted to non-combat flying and worked ferrying aircraft, parts, and supplies from one location to another.

WOMEN OF COURAGE AND CONVICTION

WASP

In July 1943, the Women Airforce Service Pilots (WASP) was formed out of two early programs that deployed female pilots. During the war, members of the WASP flew more than seventy different types of aircraft. They also flew more than sixty million miles, delivering new planes, instructing male cadet pilots, training troops for anti-aircraft gunnery, simulating bombing and strafing runs, testing new and repaired planes, breaking in new engines, delivering aircraft in need of repair to maintenance facilities, and transporting government officials within the United States.

WASP pilots were given uniforms, but because they were civilian contract employees, they had to pay for room and board at military facilities. Their civilian status also meant that the thirty-eight WASP pilots who died while performing their duties during the war were deprived of military honors. The military would not even pay to transport their remains home for burial.

HAZEL YING LEE (1912–44)

Hazel Ying Lee was a pilot who flew for the U.S. Army Air Forces during World War II. In October 1932, she became one of the first Chinese-American women to gain a pilot's license. By 1943, she was an experienced pilot and eager to join the WASP training program. On graduation, she was assigned to the delivery of aircraft to points of embarkation from where they would be shipped to the European and Pacific war fronts. On November 10, 1944, Lee was ordered to the Bell Aircraft factory at Niagara Falls to pick up a plane and deliver it to Great Falls, Montana. On landing at Great Falls, her plane was involved in a collision with another aircraft, and she was killed.

WOMEN AT WORK

"Recently, I saw women who drove long distances and worked long hours in a shipyard in New England. Most of them had made temporary arrangements for the care of their homes and children, and were working with their husbands if their husbands had not gone to war, so as to pay the mortgage on the farm, buy certain things long coveted which would make life easier in the future, or lay aside some money which would give the children some special advantages. They knew the work was temporary and feared they would never have the opportunity to achieve certain desires if they did not take advantage of the present need for workers."

Eleanor Roosevelt, August 1944

Right: A young woman tends her victory garden during World War II. This increase in domestic farming allowed more food to be diverted to the troops.

HOME AND FAMILY

With men away, life changed for all family members during the war. Women were left to make the major decisions for the family in a time of great hardship. With food rationing, women had to become creative cooks, and a scarcity of clothing meant they had to make do and mend. The shortage of nylon, which was mostly being used to make parachutes, meant that women either went without stockings or faked them by painting seams up the backs of their bare legs. Mothers and children collected and recycled items and planted "victory gardens"; any outdoor space available—in backyards, empty lots, and city rooftops—was used as a place to grow fruit and vegetables.

Many working women found the demands of holding down a job and caring for a family impossible to meet. Child-care provision for working mothers was inadequate, and commentators began to observe a rise in the numbers of "latchkey" children, delinquents, and teenage runaways. Women themselves were anxious about the health and happiness of their children. When a cross section of women were asked in 1943 whether they would take a job in a war plant if their children were looked after in day care free of charge, only 29 percent said yes, while 56 percent said no.

TROOPERS AND TRAILBLAZERS

The changing role of women in the early 1940s was reflected in the movies, where a number of female stars became renowned for their feisty, resourceful attitude to life both on- and offscreen. Actresses such as Katharine Hepburn, Joan Crawford, Bette Davis, Rosalind Russell, and Barbara Stanwyck (a self-proclaimed "tough old dame from Brooklyn") took on roles that portrayed women as independent and spirited—though they were usually brought to heel by a strong male co-star toward the end of the final reel.

This "tough gal" image contrasted with another favorite of Hollywood's at that time, where women were depicted as dutiful housewives, holding the family together while waiting for their men to come home from the war. Motherhood was promoted as the ultimate fulfillment of female identity. Magazine articles described the offscreen lives of stars such as Joan Crawford and Claudette Colbert and showed them going about their domestic chores with charm and glamour. The fact that these women earned vast sums of money in comparison with the rest of the population, and therefore could hire in all the help they needed, was neatly sidestepped.

> ❝
>
> ### WOMEN AT HOME
>
> *"[Although it is difficult to keep house all day,] take care of three children and be a bundle of charm at the day's end . . . that is what man has expected of a wife since the world began—and if you love your husband and want to keep him it would be worth your effort to try this. . . . Try to be gay and interesting when he is at home."*
>
> Movie actress Claudette Colbert, in an article titled "What Should I Do?" in the magazine *Photoplay*, June 1944

Below: In this carefully posed "informal" photo, trailblazing movie star Joan Crawford contradicts her onscreen image by presenting herself as a sweetly smiling housewife.

CHAPTER 3

THE POST-WAR WORLD

ORLD WAR II BROUGHT ABOUT A MAJOR CHANGE IN WOMEN'S economic and social status. Between 1940 and 1945, the number of working women had increased from 25 percent to 36 percent. By the war's end in 1945, nearly twenty million women had become members of the labor force. They were no longer entirely dependent on men for their keep, nor were they confined to an "invisible" role in the home, raising children. In some cases, women earned enough to support husbands who were wounded or ill.

Below: During the war, the proportion of African-American women working in factories rose from 7.3 percent to 18.6 percent.

RECOGNITION AT LAST

Women's visibility in and their contribution to the workplace meant they gained respect and were recognized as workers who had been essential to the country's survival. Public opinion had shifted toward accepting the notion of wage-earning women, even though questions were also raised about the effects on family life and the stability of society.

ALL CHANGE!

The years of depression during the 1930s, followed by the upheaval of war, had led to a deep insecurity among Americans about post-war economic prospects. As men came home from combat, the national priority was to find them jobs. The returning soldiers faced an uncertain future since everything, including the world of work and the women within it, had changed. Fear of recession and lack of jobs fueled the argument for the restoration of the family. Many Americans believed the time

"The greater social freedom of women has more or less inevitably led to a greater degree of sexual laxity, a freedom which strikes at the heart of family stability. . . . When women work, earn, and spend as much as men do, they are going to ask for equal rights with men. But the right to behave like a man [means] also the right to misbehave as he does. The decay of established moralities [comes] about as a by-product."

From *Marriage and the Family*, edited by Reuben Hill and Howard Baker, 1940

Left: The men come home: a U.S. Navy officer greets his wife and two daughters on the dock next to a navy ship after returning from duty in the Pacific.

FREEDOM AND INDEPENDENCE

"My mother warned me when I took the job that I would never be the same. She said, 'You will never want to go back to being a housewife.' At that time I didn't think it would change a thing. But she was right, it definitely did. . . . At Boeing I found a freedom and an independence that I had never known. After the war I could never go back to playing bridge again, being a club woman . . . when I knew there were things you could use your mind for. The war changed my life completely. I guess you could say, at thirty-one, I finally grew up."

Inez Sauer, who worked as a Boeing tool clerk in the war years

had come for women to return to the home and focus on rebuilding family life there.

Propaganda had worked to entice women to work during the war years, and now it sought to lure them back to domesticity. Magazines published articles insisting that women made less reliable employees than men, and arguing that they should not work if their husbands could earn enough to support them. The Selective Service Act ruled that war veterans should take priority over wartime workers in the competition for their old jobs. When peacetime came, the production

TURNING POINT

GOESAERT V. CLEARY, 1948

In the case of *Goesaert v. Cleary,* the U.S. Supreme Court upheld a law in Michigan that prohibited women from working behind a bar unless their father or husband owned the establishment. Justices Rutledge, Douglas, and Murphy argued that this was a violation of the equal protection clause of the 14th Amendment of the U.S. Constitution. Their action drew attention to the unequal treatment of women that was widespread in American society.

of war plants fell and so did job opportunities. As a result, many women were dismissed. It is estimated that two million Rosie the Riveters left their jobs at the end of World War II.

BRAVE NEW WORLD

While some women were happy to leave work and return home to the marriages they had been missing during the war years, many others were reluctant to give up their newfound independence. A 1944 study showed that 80 percent of women who had worked during the war wanted to continue in their jobs. Some members of the U.S. government argued that women who had been so invaluable to the war effort should be allowed to continue earning their own living after its end.

Meanwhile, taboos were being challenged: for example, the war seemed to have broken down the barriers to employing married women. In 1940, before the war, only 36 percent of women workers were married, compared with 50 percent in 1945. Contrary to expectations, there was an economic boom after 1947 in the United States, which resulted in a growing demand for female workers in sales and service jobs. Women were also needed to fill positions as typists, teachers, and nurses and in manufacturing and industry.

FEMALE PROFESSIONALS

The post-war world also showed signs that women were at last beginning to break into the world of the male professions: for example, Harvard Medical School admitted women for the first time in 1945, Margaret Chase Smith became the first woman elected to both houses of Congress in 1948, and Burnita Shelton Matthews was named Federal District Court judge for the District of Columbia in 1949. In contrast, in an article in the *Saturday Evening Post* in 1948, Susan B. Anthony IV remarked on the decrease

Left: Republican senator Margaret Chase Smith (1897–1995) had a strong interest in the military and was at the forefront of the struggle to win permanent status for women in the armed services.

Above: Judge Burnita Shelton Matthews (1894–1988) helped form organizations such as the Woman's Bar Association of the District of Columbia and the National Association of Women Lawyers to represent the interests of professional women.

> ## BREAKTHROUGH BIOGRAPHY
>
> ### CLARE BOOTHE LUCE (1903–87)
>
> Clare Boothe Luce was a diplomat, politician, and author. She worked her way out of a poverty-stricken childhood to become one of the most successful and admired women of her time. Two successive marriages to wealthy businessmen helped her political and artistic ambitions. Luce worked as a war correspondent at the start of World War II, publishing articles for *Life* magazine and a nonfiction memoir, *Europe in the Spring*, in 1940. She served as a congressional representative for Connecticut from 1942 to 1946. In 1953, she became the first female ambassador to a major nation when President Dwight D. Eisenhower appointed her the U.S. ambassador to Italy. Luce was a staunch Republican for most of her life. On her death, she left most of her $70 million estate to help the careers of women in science and engineering.

in the number of women lawyers and school superintendents. A stark reminder of the lack of professional opportunities for women could be seen in medical schools, which operated a quota system that restricted female admissions to just 5 percent.

UNEQUAL RIGHTS

In addition to receiving only restricted access to higher-paid professional work, women's wages generally remained lower than men's. Despite the fact that a new generation of female labor reformers had emerged, prepared to fight for economic and gender equality, they still found it impossible to push the long-debated Equal Rights Amendment through Congress. This meant there was no legislation to prevent women from being demoted to lower-paid jobs or blocked for promotion. The male-

Below: During World War II, the number of women joining labor unions quadrupled. In May 1941, female union members outside a mill in Greensboro, Greene County, Georgia, jeer at workers who are breaking a strike.

dominated unions, which had supported some equal pay measures during the war, reverted to their practice of reserving higher-paying positions for men.

BACKLASH

Despite the important work that women had done during the war years, the majority of Americans still believed that wives should not work if their husbands could support them. Sociologist Willard Waller argued that during the war, women had "gotten out of hand" and they now displayed a willful independence that threatened the welfare of children and the family. Fears of adultery among women whose men were fighting overseas, whether well founded or not, were widespread. The media were quick to exploit these fears, and 1940s movies were peppered with representations of "dangerous" man-eating females, or *femmes fatales*, whose presence meant nothing but trouble.

Servicemen often found the return to civilian life very difficult since their wives and children had become strangers to them during the years of separation. The horrors and stresses that soldiers had experienced during the war made matters worse. Many couples had married in haste, at the outbreak of war, and subsequently found they were incompatible. A post-war housing shortage meant that families often had to live with relatives or in cramped, one-room apartments, which placed additional strain on relationships. Between 1940 and 1945,

Left: In the movie *Double Indemnity* (1944), Barbara Stanwyck plays the evil seductress Phyllis Dietrichson, a role that demonstrates all the qualities of a *femme fatale.* The ruthless Phyllis uses her sexuality and wit to engineer the murder of her husband in order to claim an insurance policy on his life.

> ## LOOKING HAPPY
>
> "Listen to your laughter. . . . Let it come easily, especially if you're with boys who have had little to laugh at for too long. Laugh at the silly things you used to do together. . . . And if you hear your laugh sound hysterical, giddy or loud, tone it down. . . . Serenity is the wellspring of the romantic look. . . . This Christmas, with our men home, surely we should know serenity. So let us look happy and contented and starry-eyed."
>
> Model and actress Anita Colby gives some specific advice to female readers in an article titled "That Romantic Look," *Photoplay,* December 1946

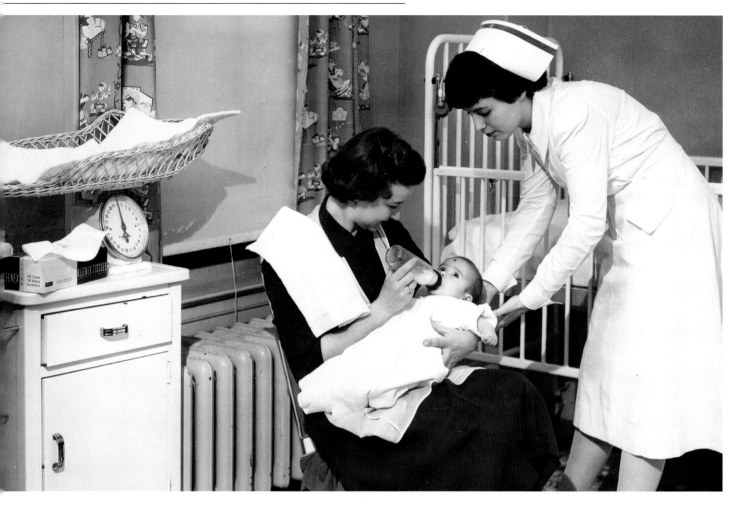

Above: In the 1940s, childlessness was widely regarded as selfish and deviant. A 1946 issue of *Newsweek* magazine ran an article claiming that the education of women was bad for fertility: "For the American girl books and babies don't mix."

TURNING POINT

TACKLING EXPLOITATION

In 1949, the United Nations adopted the Convention for the Suppression of the Traffic in Persons and of the Exploitation of the Prostitution of Others. This condemned prostitution and required U.N. member nations to monitor all ports to prevent the traffic of women and children across international borders. The convention was a major landmark in the battle to eliminate the exploitation of women and vulnerable younger people.

the rate of divorce rose from sixteen to twenty-seven per hundred marriages. By 1950, as many as a million ex-servicemen were divorced.

CHILD CARE AND CHILDBIRTH

During the war, the federal government spent about $52 million on 3,102 day-care centers for the children of working mothers. After the war, the government withdrew support for these centers, believing them to be unnecessary now that women were no longer essential to the workforce. This measure hit low-income families particularly hard since most of them could not earn a living wage unless the mothers worked.

Birthrates soared at the end of the war, suggesting that women were choosing motherhood over employment and higher education. Despite the fact that women's opportunities had been significantly expanded during the war years, traditional attitudes toward a woman's place in society remained largely unchanged—her primary role was to stay home and raise children.

However, the way women gave birth had undergone a major transformation. With advances in medical science, by the mid-20th century home births were seen as dangerous and primitive. By 1940, the majority of women were giving birth in hospital, under the supervision of specialists who administered a cocktail of drugs both during labor and to induce it.

DEFYING CONVENTION

Despite the fact that the post-war world appeared to favor stay-at-home moms, some women remained active in the workplace. In politics, the intrepid and socially committed Eleanor Roosevelt was, in 1945, appointed by President Harry S. Truman to serve on the U.S. delegation to the United Nations. In 1948, she presented the Universal Declaration of Human Rights to the U.N. General Assembly for adoption. On a less elevated level, there were also women involved in the labor movement, lobbying for industrial rights. They included Ruth Young, Luisa Moreno, Mary Callahan, Addie Wyatt, and Myra Wolfgang.

THE ARTS

In 1942, Viola Smith, a drummer with seventeen years of experience, was quoted in music magazine *Down Beat* talking about the existence of "hep girls," female jazz musicians "who could sit in any jam session and hold their own." Her assertion prompted a flurry of letters to the editor debating the question: Can women play jazz? Elsewhere artists, including Lee Krasner and Elaine de Kooning, explored new forms such as abstract expressionism and writers such as Eudora Welty and Kay Boyle examined the social and moral aspects of the times they lived in.

WOMEN OF COURAGE AND CONVICTION

BETTE DAVIS (1908–89)

Bette Davis was one of Hollywood's most successful actresses, and among its most confrontational. In 1937, when she tried to free herself from her contract with Warner Brothers, the press portrayed her as overpaid and ungrateful. Davis lost her battle with Warner Brothers but began to earn the respect of the studio bosses. Her career, which involved playing forceful and often unsympathetic characters, went from strength to strength. In 1941, she became the first female president of the Academy of Motion Picture Arts and Sciences, and by 1942, she was the highest-paid woman in America. Her personal life was troubled: she underwent three divorces and brought up her children as a single parent. The inscription on her tombstone reads: "She did it the hard way."

Below: Bette Davis was famous for standing up to studio executives and movie directors.

CHAPTER 4

DAILY LIFE IN THE 1950S

T HE UNITED STATES EMERGED FROM WORLD WAR II the richest and most powerful nation on earth. People's relief that the war was over was expressed in a desire to withdraw from the wider world. One way of doing this was to take refuge in a fulfilling private life in a suburban home with a white picket fence and backyard barbecue. Managing a home and rearing a family became the goal of most women during the 1950s.

Below: 1950s teenage dating rules were strict. Girls were encouraged to develop social skills and charm to attract a boy. Once they were "going steady," it was up to the girl to keep the boy at arm's length until he proposed marriage.

THE SEARCH FOR STABILITY

During the decade, a huge increase occurred in couples getting married and marrying younger. Marriage rates were much higher, for example, than in Europe, still mired in post-war austerity. By the end of the 1950s, 70 percent of women had married by age twenty-four, compared to 42 percent in 1940. This was an era of relative stability in marriage, with a lower divorce rate than in any other decade of the 20th century.

Because marriage, certainly for women, was now the main aim in life, dating became more important than ever. Courtship between boy and girl was a formal process with an elaborate set of rules. A wealth of advice was available in women's magazines. These publications encouraged their female readers' obsession with allure, giving fashion, beauty, and behavior tips on "how to catch a husband" or, more ominously for the man concerned, "how to snare a male."

GOING STEADY

A period of dating, or "going steady," came before marriage. During this time, the boy would give the girl some token, such as a class ring or letter sweater, and was expected to call her a certain number of times and take her on a certain number of dates each week. Neither boy nor girl was allowed to date anyone else. The greater physical intimacy implied by going steady meant that the burden of "drawing the line" in terms of sexual activity was borne by girls, who were expected to "save themselves" for marriage. Although going steady was no guarantee of marriage, the desire for security with an exclusive partner at as young an age as was legal was a feature of the 1950s.

MARRIAGE

Getting married straight out of high school or while in college was considered the norm. It was commonly believed that it was far more important to nail a husband than a college degree. If a woman wasn't engaged or married by her early twenties, she was thought to be in danger of becoming an "old maid." Once married, couples tended to start families right away. With home life idealized as "domestic bliss"

Below: Early marriage was the aim for most women. The authors of a 1950s lifestyle book offered the following reassurance: "If you are more than 23 years old ... perhaps you have begun to wonder whether Mr. Right would ever come along for you. Your chances are still good...."

MIXED MESSAGE

"My father expected me to get an 'A' in every subject, [but] my mother says, 'Don't become so deep that no man will be good enough for you.'"

A female college student quoted in *Women in the Modern World: Their Education and Their Dilemmas* by Mirra Komarovsky

BEING A WOMAN

"What modern woman has to recapture is the wisdom that just being a woman is her central task and her greatest honor. . . . Women must boldly announce that no job is more exacting, more necessary, or more rewarding than that of housewife and mother."

Agnes Meyer in an article "Women Aren't Men," *Atlantic* magazine, August 1950

"

NORMAL BEHAVIOR

"People who voluntarily refrain from having children are deviating from normal behavior."

Ferdinand Lundberg and Marynia Farnham, *Modern Woman: The Lost Sex,* 1947

Right: The baby boom was the result of early marriage and social pressure to conform to the nuclear family.

TURNING POINT

THE PILL

In 1951, the Planned Parenthood Federation gave a tiny grant to scientist Gregory Pincus to develop a hormonal contraceptive pill. In the same year, a chemist named Carl Djerassi, working in Mexico City, created an orally effective form of progesterone pill. The actual chemistry of the pill was invented there in Mexico, but neither Djerassi nor the company he worked for was interested in testing it as a contraceptive. In 1953, Pincus received a substantial grant enabling him to continue his work. He joined forces with John Rock, another scientist working in the field, and together they tested the drug on fifty female patients. The birth-control pill did not become widely available until the early 1960s, when it had a major impact on the biological and social lives of women.

and the virtues of the nuclear family celebrated, there was little reason to delay.

BABY BOOM

The fear of a decrease in population as a result of the war led U.S. government officials and scientists to call for a return to large families. Now parenthood was seen as part of being a responsible citizen. During the baby boom between 1940 and 1960, the birthrate doubled for third children and tripled for fourth children.

COLD WAR FEARS

The pressure on American women to have babies was partly a terrified reaction to the threat posed by the Cold War and nuclear weapons. Although the end of World War II brought peace, it also created a heightened state of tension between the world's two military superpowers, the Soviet Union and the United States. America was afraid that the Soviet Union planned to export its style of government—communism—to other nations. The United States saw this as a threat to its democratic system and focused its efforts on preventing the spread of communism, both at home and abroad. This approach to foreign policy led to its involvement in the Korean War (1950–53), the first armed conflict of the Cold War.

The atom bombs dropped on Hiroshima and Nagasaki at the end of World War II had proved the devastating power of nuclear weapons. With the development of the even more powerful H-bomb in 1952 and intercontinental missile systems to deliver it, nations soon had the power to wipe out millions of people at the push of a button. From the 1950s on, the two superpowers competed in a race to build up stocks of nuclear weapons until both countries had the power to destroy each other many times over. This nuclear threat led to intense anxiety in the general population.

THE CONVENTIONAL FAMILY

These developments in the early 1950s produced a society that was conservative in its views and lifestyle. Although more women were going out to work, commentators argued that true female contentment

Below: Family and children were the chief focus of most women's lives in the 1950s. Motherhood was the main source of a woman's identity.

Above: The 1950s suburban dream was a comfortable, detached family home with driveway, lawn, and garage, like this house in Crookston, Minnesota.

THE GOAL OF MARRIAGE

"*A career is just fine, but it's no substitute for marriage. Don't you think a man is the most important thing in the world? A woman isn't a woman until she's been married and had children.*"

Debbie Reynolds in the movie *The Tender Trap*, 1955

could be found only in the home. Their cause was taken up by writers in magazines such as *McCall's* and *Ladies Home Journal*. Women were urged to stop "aping" male behavior and to revive the lost arts of canning fruit, and interior decorating. The conventional family consisted of distinct roles for men and women: a breadwinner father, a full-time homemaker mother, and three or four dependent children.

SUBURBIA

Economic prosperity created a boom in suburban housing. Spurred on by images of domestic bliss promoted by magazines and movies, young newlyweds dreamed of moving out of cramped city apartments and into commuter-belt homes of their own. New, affordable houses were built on the edges of cities to accommodate this dream. Between 1950 and 1968, commuter areas grew more than five times faster than urban areas. Ranch-style houses, each with its own patch of lawn, sprang up across the United States. Between 1948 and 1958, thirteen million homes were built, 85 percent of them in the suburbs.

A BLUEPRINT FOR LIVING

The suburban way of life shaped the pattern of the American family. Because men most likely had to commute to and from a job in a city center, they were usually absent from the home. Tucked away in her well-equipped kitchen, the typical housewife worked hard to make the home an oasis of calm for her overworked husband. She was expected to have a meal on the table and pour him a drink, while lending a sympathetic ear to his troubles when he returned from work. During the day, her main focus was the children. She was responsible for playing with and disciplining them, and ferrying them to and from school, friends' houses, and music lessons in the family station wagon. In her spare hours, she might volunteer for the school parent-teacher association or library.

Fewer suburban wives and mothers worked than their urban counterparts. Jobs were limited, and domestic help was in short supply. With little stimulating contact with other adults, this way of life often led to isolation, boredom, and loneliness. Tupperware parties, which a housewife could host in order to sell a new brand of plastic container to friends and neighbors, were one way to pass the time, meet with other adults, and earn a little money.

TOGETHERNESS

Nevertheless, family life in the suburbs represented security in an insecure world. Protected from the labor unrest and racial tensions in the cities, the virtually all-white suburbs provided a safe if bland way of being. The importance of family "togetherness" emphasized by women's magazines meant that "creative" activities such as camping trips and barbecues in the backyard became fashionable weekend pursuits. If families had any time left to spare, they could spend it stocking the pantries of their home-based bomb shelters so they would be prepared in the event of a Soviet nuclear attack.

COLD WAR GAMES

"*Civil defense training is almost akin to religious training. . . . We must teach our children protection. . . . A mother must calm the fears of her child. Make a game out of it: Playing Civil Defense.*"

From Jean Wood Fuller's "Wisdom Is Defense" address before the state meeting of Women in Civil Defense, Richmond Hotel, Augusta, Georgia, November 10, 1954

Below: In 1955, a family tests out the "Kidde Kokoon," an underground bomb shelter manufactured by Walter Kidde Nuclear Laboratories of Garden City, Long Island.

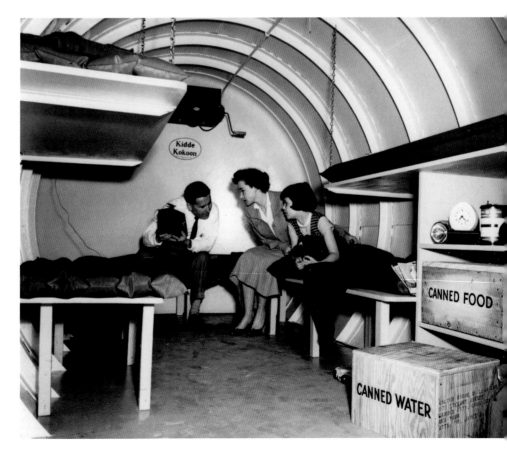

Above: The impact of suburban life on consumer behavior was significant. People took pride in filling their nice homes with new gadgets such as washing machines and refrigerators.

READY MEALS

"Life (they keep telling us) is due to grow ever brighter and easier for women in 1958. In the do-it-yourself era, women have learned that it's possible to prepare and serve a company dinner after spending a full day at an office job, with the aid of modern frozen, ready-mixed and prepared packaged foods. . . . The next step in the spare-the-housewife movement, says manufacturer Victor Muscat, is the scheduled appearance on the market next year of all kinds of food in aluminum packages. . . . He foresees the day when whole meals will come neatly prepared, packaged and ready to squirt, squeeze or zip, heat and eat . . . when there will be no dishes to wash, no pans to scour and a housewife's life at last will be a merry one."

Rocky Mount Evening Telegram, December 17, 1957

TECHNOLOGICAL ADVANCES

The suburban home became a shrine to consumerism since owning the latest modern item or piece of furniture was a badge of success for hardworking families. New kitchen appliances, such as automatic washing machines, clothes dryers, freezers, and electric mixers, made housewifery appear more "glamorous." In theory, the drudgery of women's lives was eased by these "laborsaving" gadgets, but in reality, 1950s middle-class housewives had less paid help than previous generations and therefore did more washing, cooking, and shopping. To make matters worse, the wife was left with little to show for her efforts: because housework was regarded as menial, a woman's social status was determined by her husband's job, not by her own achievements.

MENTAL HEALTH

The anxiety that colored the 1950s political scene extended to attitudes toward child rearing. The early part of the decade was the last period during which large numbers of children fell victim to serious childhood illnesses such as polio. Parents therefore watched their children closely to identify any symptom that might suggest the onset of a dreaded disease. Because young suburban wives were often isolated from the help and support of their extended families, they turned to child-care books for assistance. In many cases, these were counsels of perfection, placing the responsibility for healthy child development solely on the mother.

The stresses on women caused by pressure to conform to a rigid ideal meant that the successful 1950s family was often achieved at enormous cost to the wife. She was required always to put her husband and children before her own needs, and this led to brooding resentment, discontentment, and, in more serious cases, alcoholism and dependence on barbiturates and tranquilizers. During the 1950s, a boom occurred in the number of women seeking psychotherapy. Expectations that women should be fulfilled by motherhood meant that anxiety about pregnancy was considered a mental illness. Women displaying mental distress at the narrow role allotted to them were often prescribed drugs to lessen the symptoms. The most extreme cases were confined in psychiatric institutions where they were given electric shock treatments. As a result of this, understandably, the freedoms offered by the 1960s were readily embraced by many 1950s housewives and their daughters.

COMPLICATED RELATIONSHIPS

"I liked the members of our Women's Commission personally, but I felt they were not typical women and knew little of the problems of ordinary women. They were political career-women, without husbands and children. . . . I knew that . . . I was no truly emancipated, independent Woman, but I felt that the whole issue was more complicated than that of holding an outside job or having an independent career. Human relationships, and certainly male–female relationships, were more complicated than our Party could admit."

Peggy Dennis, *The Autobiography of an American Communist: A Personal View of a Political Life, 1925–1975*. Describing her experiences as a Communist Party member and as a wife and mother, Peggy Dennis argues that childless career women did not understand the complexities of trying to combine work with family commitments.

Right: In the 2007 TV series *Mad Men*, housewife Betty Draper (January Jones) appears to have it all—a handsome husband, and a perfect home and family. However, boredom and frustration with her suburban life lead her to seek psychiatric help.

CHAPTER 5

WORK AND THE 1950S WOMAN

D URING THE 1950S, MORE AND MORE WOMEN ENTERED THE LABOR force, so that by 1960, one in three wives worked outside the home. Most of them were over the age of thirty-five, with older children, and very few of them pursued careers. The majority held part-time "pink-collar" jobs as salesclerks, secretaries, or bank tellers and used their incomes to help put children through college, pay off the mortgage, or pay for a family vacation. Women's work was, in general, secondary both in status and in pay to that of men, and their earnings were regarded as "pin money." Nevertheless, many women who worked said they enjoyed higher self-esteem than if they did not work outside the home.

"

WOMEN'S RIGHTS

"Where is our democracy in this country if a woman cannot be a free individual and make up her own mind? I think that when you start telling women you can or cannot work, you are infringing upon their civil rights which I, as a woman, resent."

Mildred Szur, union delegate, from "Women Workers Win 'Battle of the Sexes' at United Automobile Workers Convention," March 31, 1955

Right: In 1953 in Greenville, South Carolina, a female operative mends a yarn break on a quilling machine. Many women were eager to work so they could afford a better standard of living, but they also valued their jobs for the opportunity to be with other people and gain recognition for their work.

JOB RIGHTS

The campaign for women's job rights had started among "blue-collar" (manual) workers earlier in the century. Women in this sector had joined unions, gaining a powerful channel through which they could express their concerns. Somewhat surprisingly, working-class women workers tended to have more of a voice than their middle-class equivalents. By the mid-1950s, a number of unions had made real progress in tackling sex discrimination in the hiring, laying off, and promotion of female workers. However, it was not the case that women automatically supported one another: a slump in industry in the early 1950s meant that single women (as well as men) criticized married women who worked for taking jobs they did not need.

While part-time work suited the lifestyle of many middle-class wives and mothers, women employed in the pink-collar sector tended not to be unionized. They had virtually no rights, and many were hired on

WOMEN OF COURAGE AND CONVICTION

JACQUELINE COCHRAN (1906–80)

Born into poverty in Florida, Cochran started her career as a beautician. Marriage to a wealthy businessman enabled her to pursue a career as an aviatrix. She learned to fly with only three weeks' training and earned a commercial pilot's license before she was thirty. During World War II, she helped deliver American-built planes to Britain. In 1950, she set a new speed record for propeller-driven aircraft, and in 1953, she became the first woman to break the sound barrier, flying a Canadian Air Force Sabrejet at an average speed of 652 miles (1,050 kilometers) per hour.

Left: Pilot Jacqueline Cochran stands in the cockpit of her jet aircraft after becoming the first woman to travel at the speed of sound.

WOMAN POWER

"Today, when so much depends on our ability to out-produce the Russians, the fullest employment of trained womanpower has become a vital factor in the Cold War."

From an article in the
American Federationist, 1955

the basis of their physical attractiveness alone. In the early 1950s, "white-collar" jobs, including those of teacher and airline stewardess, tended to be reserved for young, white, single women. It was common to fire married women if they became pregnant. In the airlines, it was also general practice to "retire" female employees when they reached their early thirties because they were thought to be less attractive to male passengers after this age. One business executive remarked: "Put a dog on a plane and twenty businessmen are sore for a month."

THE POLITICAL MOOD

At the end of World War II, Europe was divided between the communist East, allied to the Soviet Union, and the liberal-democratic West, allied to the United States. This division, known as the "Iron Curtain," was both physical and cultural. Lydia Kirk, a journalist for *Life* magazine, visited Moscow in the early 1950s and filed a report on Soviet women's fashion. She described the styles as dowdy and shapeless and saw Soviet women as oppressed, unlike their contemporaries in the democratic United States. This mix of scorn and fear of the Soviet Union colored American attitudes throughout the 1950s.

The wave of anti-communism that swept the United States cost many women—and men—their jobs. The mood reached fever pitch during the administration of President Harry S. Truman when the House Committee on Un-American Activities (HUAC) was set up to root out people suspected of having communist beliefs. Republican senator Joseph McCarthy led the witch hunts with great determination and

ON THIS AMERICAN MODEL AND HANGING ALONGSIDE HER IS A COMPLETE AND STYLISH SOVIET WARDROBE, THE TOTAL COST, EXCLUDING HAT, IS $461.40

IRON CURTAIN LOOK IS HERE

U.S. ENVOY'S WIFE FINDS MOSCOW MODES HIGH PRICED, WIDE SHOULDERED, NOT VERY HANDSOME

The slender gams of the girl above give her away as American. The clothes are not. They are new Soviet styles brought home by Mrs. Alan G. Kirk, wife of the recent U.S. ambassador. Here is almost the entire wardrobe for an Iron Curtain look as decreed by Soviet designers. Displayed in Bonwit Teller's, New York, the Moscow modes excited most interest by their cost, translated from rubles: suit $126, dress $128, coat $155, shoes $14.50, bag $19.80, gloves $18.10.

To an American the handsomest garment was the traditional fur hat, which is not considered particularly chic in the U.S.S.R. The rest, drab and stiff, did not do much for the model. They might have done even less had she also worn the other two staples of the wardrobe, an anatomically unique bra, shaped like a double-barrelled shotgun, and knitted bloomers of a shade one observer calls "MVD blue" because it is the color of a Russian secret policeman's cap.

CONTINUED ON NEXT PAGE 119

Left: In 1952, despite the wave of anti-communist feeling engulfing the United States, *Life* magazine predicted that Soviet fashion could take hold in the West.

Right: In October 1947, a group of Hollywood movie stars flew from Los Angeles to Washington, D.C., to protest the manner in which the United States government's investigation of "un-American activities" was being conducted. They are, left to right, front row: Geraldine Brooks, June Havoc, Marsha Hunt, Lauren Bacall, Richard Conte, and Evelyn Keyes; left to right, back row: Paul Henreid, Humphrey Bogart, Gene Kelly, and Danny Kaye.

energy. Workers in the film industry, education, labor unions, and the government were investigated. People were expected to inform on their colleagues ("to name names") or face the possibility of a jail sentence or being blacklisted so they could not get a job. Thousands of people were suddenly refused work, among them many women, including writer Dorothy Parker, actresses Dolores del Rio, Ruth Gordon, and Lee Grant, singer Lena Horne, and playwright Lillian Hellman.

The conservative nature of 1950s America meant that women who dared to deviate from the norm of wife and homemaker were criticized. People who simply drew attention to inequalities in society were often accused of being communists. When Simone de Beauvoir's groundbreaking examination of the treatment of women throughout history, *The Second Sex*, was published in the United States in 1953, some commentators cited her left-wing politics as evidence that her ideas could not be trusted.

A MAN'S WORLD

The Cold War meant that national security and foreign policy were a major focus of political life. The top government jobs were all held by men, typically with a background in business, law, or banking, and for whom toughness was a virtue. These men operated in an environment where feminine qualities seemed out of place. Women were regarded as weak and in need of male protection, not interested in learning and doing the same things as men. Confusingly, they were not seen as weak but praised when it came to doing work that

WOMEN OF COURAGE AND CONVICTION

MARGARET CHASE SMITH (1897–1995)

Senator Margaret Chase Smith came to national attention on June 1, 1950, when she spoke out against the tactics of fellow Republican senator Joseph McCarthy. In her "Declaration of Conscience" speech to Congress, Smith defended the people's freedom of belief and speech and spoke out against McCarthy's bullying campaign.

Left: In the 1959 romantic comedy *Pillow Talk*, successful career girl Doris Day is eventually won over by charmer Rock Hudson.

contributed to the national good and supported the Cold War economy. Such mixed messages regarding the role of women were typical of the time.

MOVIES

In the movies of the 1950s, the career woman replaced the 1940s seductress as the *femme fatale*. Women who selfishly neglected their husbands and children to pursue a life of work outside the home were shown as the root of society's ills, leading to juvenile delinquency, social breakdown, and crime. In *A Star Is Born* (1954), Judy Garland's husband pays the ultimate price for his wife's success—suicide. It was acceptable for a girl to work before she married, however. This was borne out by movies starring sensible girl-next-door types such as Doris Day (*Pillow Talk*) and Debbie Reynolds (*The Tender Trap*), who were happy to abandon their successful careers when they found Mr. Right.

THE ADVERTISING INVASION

In the 1950s, the media invaded people's private space in a way it never had before. Suddenly every home had a television and family evenings were spent grouped around it. Television replaced movies as the dominant form of entertainment. Notions of how women should look and behave were increasingly shaped by television, and advertisers lost no time in making use of this new medium to sell products. For most middle-class families, the husband's paycheck alone could not buy the wealth of goods advertisers told them they needed to maintain or enhance their quality of life. Many women

TURNING POINT

ALL-WOMEN RADIO

On October 29, 1955, WHER, the first all-women radio station, went on the air in Memphis, Tennessee. At WHER, women read the news, interviewed local celebrities, and played records. Behind the scenes, they sold and created commercials, produced and directed programming, and sat at the station's control boards. WHER was the brainchild of record producer Sam Phillips, who said in 1960: "When I started WHER ... people thought I had rocks in my head. A girl could do a cooking show, but no one thought girls could handle hour-to-hour programs and commercials. I felt differently. I had always wanted a radio station, but Memphis already had nine. I had to do something different. An all-girl crew, and pleasant, light music, was the answer."

therefore returned to work to supplement the family income so they could enjoy "the American standard of living."

FAMILY LIFE AS SEEN ON TV

The middle-class family had its image boosted by a host of TV situation comedies in which the issue of how to raise children was addressed. Fictional families such as the Andersons (*Father Knows Best*), the Cleavers (*Leave It to Beaver*), and the Stones (*The Donna Reed Show*) showed mothers holding home life together while their husbands worked. Blue-collar audiences were offered tales of families struggling to better themselves and climb the economic ladder (*The Honeymooners* and *I Love Lucy*). In *I Love Lucy*, a usually ditzy housewife (Lucille

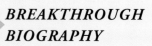

BREAKTHROUGH BIOGRAPHY

LUCILLE BALL (1911–89)

In spite of her scatterbrained onscreen persona, the real-life Lucille Ball was a show-business powerhouse and television pioneer. With her husband, Desi Arnaz, she co-owned one of the most successful television production studios in history and introduced the idea of syndicating programs. Their situation comedy, *I Love Lucy*, was launched in 1951 after Ball had convinced television network CBS to sign over the rights and creative control to herself and Arnaz. When Ball became pregnant, her condition was written into the script and millions of viewers watched fascinated as the story unfolded on TV.

Left: Real-life and onscreen husband and wife Desi Arnaz and Lucille Ball starred in the hit TV comedy show *I Love Lucy*.

Above: Images of bombshells were used to decorate aircraft and boost the morale of servicemen during World War II.

Ball) could call on her instinctive female common sense to keep her husband's wilder ambitions in check.

BOMBSHELLS

While women were expected to act as agents of social control, helping to instill values into men and children, it was also believed that women themselves needed to be controlled, both inside and outside the home. In the society of the time, the term "bombshell" came to be used to describe a sexually attractive woman. Blond bombshells, such as Marilyn Monroe and Jayne Mansfield, featured in Hollywood movies and were instant style icons. After the atom bomb explosions at the end of World War II, the word "bombshell" took on extra significance, linking the idea of a sexy woman with the threat of the bomb. Like atomic power, the woman needed to be "tamed."

MOMS

Another theory about out-of-control women was put forward by college professor Philip Wylie in 1942. He described what he saw as an unhealthy obsession with the role of the mother in American society. He called this fixation "Momism." In no other country of the world, he argued, was mother worship so intense. Celebrated by politicians, Mom had a public holiday devoted to her and inspired marching bands to spell her name in formation. Hugely powerful in the home, yet frustrated with her lot in life, Mom invested everything in her children, and her smothering behavior prevented them from growing into independent adults.

CONTRADICTORY PERCEPTIONS

The rules governing female behavior were rooted in contradiction. Women continued to enter the job market to earn money to help maintain the standard of living promoted by the media. But the "masculine woman" who worked and was independent was regarded as dangerous. This conflict was a source of confusion and unhappiness for women. Also, despite the popular myth, not all American families shared in the suburban, consumerist dream. A quarter of Americans—between forty and fifty million people—were poor in the mid-1950s.

It seemed that whatever they did, women were criticized: if they worked, they were neglectful; if they stayed at home, they became domineering monsters. No wonder that when in 1960 the magazine *Redbook* ran an article titled "Why Young Mothers Feel Trapped," it received 24,000 replies from anxious female readers.

Left: Mom worship: mothers stand in line beneath the American flag during Mother's Day celebrations on a U.S. Army base.

TURNING POINT

A LIST OF RIGHTS FOR WOMEN

Eleanor Roosevelt chaired the United Nations Commission on Human Rights and, in 1948, helped to pass the Universal Declaration of Human Rights. However, she thought more was needed to enforce equal political rights for women worldwide. She wrote a document titled "U.N. Deliberations on Draft Convention on the Political Rights of Women" (1953) in which she described what could be achieved. On March 31, 1953, U.N. delegates passed the Convention on the Political Rights of Women, which took effect on July 7, 1954.

A WOMAN'S PLACE

"There are people who say a woman's place is in the home. No one can say where anyone's place is. I say a woman's place is everywhere. No longer is she content to be told she is a second class citizen."

Caroline Davis, director, United Automobile Workers (UAW) Women's Department, c. 1955

CHAPTER 6

YOUTH, EDUCATION, AND ACHIEVEMENTS

THE RULES GOVERNING AMERICAN SOCIETY IN THE 1950S were strict yet confusing. This meant that while many adults preached a certain type of behavior, they found its standards impossible to live up to in practice. A reaction to this stifling conformity, and to the double standards of adults, was the rebellious teenager. Suddenly parents found themselves excluded from the secret adolescent world of "cool" clothing and slang phrases. Meanwhile, the conventional mainstream saw higher education institutions experiencing an increase in courses that taught young women how to become homemakers.

Below: One of the ways teenagers expressed their newfound freedom was through dances such as the jitterbug.

THE BIRTH OF THE TEENAGER

Before World War II, the majority of people, apart from the very rich, had to take life seriously from an early age, either preparing to go out to work or practicing becoming a homemaker. In the booming economy of the mid-1950s, younger people gained a great deal of economic power, freedom, and independence. Compared to their parents, girls and boys socialized more and at a younger age, going on dates, dancing to the new rock and roll and kissing at drive-in movies.

For the first time since the 1920s, young people developed their tastes and personalities outside the family, creating their own clothing, hairstyle trends, and vocabulary of slang terms, such as "cool" and "hip." The new media of TV and AM radio gave them access to a wider world of cultural influence. They often found the views of their peers more appealing than those of their parents, and this could be a source of friction at home. Teen birthrates soared in 1950s, although the high incidence of illegitimate births was masked by the practice of putting the babies of unwed mothers up for adoption.

HIGHER EDUCATION

At the end of World War II, colleges and universities experienced tremendous growth. This was largely the result of the Serviceman's Readjustment Act of 1944 (commonly known as the GI Bill), which offered college or vocational education for returning soldiers. More than six million war veterans entered higher education or other training programs. Women enrolled at college after the war, but in much lower numbers than men. There were also fewer of them enrolling than in earlier generations: in 1950, women made up only 30 percent of enrolled college students, compared with 47 percent in 1920.

THE MARRIAGE MARKET

In keeping with the climate of the time, the 1950s female student population was preoccupied with early marriage and having

Below: Urged to be competitive on the one hand and quiet and restrained on the other, 1950s college girls were often confused about how to approach their studies.

CRISIS AT COLLEGE

"For those last ten years I felt increasingly that something had gone wrong with our young women of college age. . . . I noted it all with growing alarm and anger. . . . I thought when I started teaching that since the battle to open doors to women had been won, all that was needed was for us to buckle down and show what stuff we were made of. I think I was confident the will was there—I knew the capacity was. But I was mistaken about the will."

A professor of English at the University of Illinois describes her female students of the late 1940s and early 1950s in a letter to feminist author Betty Friedan, written in 1963

TURNING POINT

AMERICAN BANDSTAND

Starting out as a local television program in Philadelphia in 1952, *American Bandstand* aired nationally in 1957 and ran for thirty-three years. The show included performances by pop musicians and featured ordinary teenagers dancing to chart music and showing off all the newest fashions. Beamed into millions of homes by the new medium of television, *American Bandstand* included dancing contests, which demonstrated "undiscovered professional talent." Teenage girls watched avidly to see the latest fashions, hairstyles, and dance moves to copy. Each week, teenagers lined up to take part, and many of the same dancers attended each Saturday, which meant that viewers became familiar with them and interested in their relationships.

Right: Unusually for its time, the 1950 movie *Born Yesterday* charts the journey of Billie Dawn (Judy Holliday) from "dumb broad" to woman of learning.

BREAKTHROUGH BIOGRAPHY

BARBARA McCLINTOCK (1902–92)

Born in Hartford, Connecticut, Barbara McClintock was for many years a leading scientist at various North American universities. From the late 1920s, she studied chromosomes and how they change during reproduction in maize (corn). She produced the first genetic "map" for maize, linking parts of the chromosome with physical traits. In 1941, she joined the staff of the Carnegie Institution of Washington, where she studied mutation (the process of change) in kernels of maize. In 1951, she discovered certain genetic elements that could move around to different positions within the genome of a single cell. These are called transposons, or jumping genes. Although her ideas were largely ignored by the scientific establishment of the time, it has since been proved that genes are responsible for switching physical characteristics on and off. Transposons are the basis of much of today's research in genetic engineering.

children. Some "experts" actually saw education for women as a hindrance to reproducing and argued that girls should focus on starting families rather than getting a college education. Whereas for a man a degree was likely to lead to a well-paid job or career, this was not the case for a woman; the female drop-out rate from college was therefore quite high.

College became the place where white girls could meet highly educated men with good job prospects and, ideally, better themselves by making a "good" marriage. Whichever way they turned, home and hearth seemed to beckon. Interestingly, black women tended to be more motivated. They expected to have to find employment, as their mothers had before them, so although they were few in number at college, they usually completed their degrees.

HOME ECONOMICS

Having had their expectations raised by college, many young women felt frustrated when, on graduation, these hopes were not fulfilled. One way to get around this problem was for colleges to tailor their curricula to prepare women more suitably for their future lives as housewives. Many female undergraduates themselves requested that the more "feminine" subjects of homemaking and motherhood be taught. As a result, there was a huge increase in home economics courses and programs. Women's instincts were generally thought to be practical rather than intellectual, so they were encouraged to study the

TRAINING HOMEMAKERS

"If [homemaking] roles are to be played with distinction, the college years must be rehearsal periods for the major performance."

James Madison Wood, president of Stephens College, Missouri

Left: Preparing for their lives in the home: an all-female class of Cornell University home economics students is taught the different elements of the iron and the proper maintenance of the tool.

applied arts such as ceramics, weaving, textiles, leatherwork, and flower arranging. Some educationalists believed that the task of creating a good home and raising good children should be treated as a profession and made the main purpose of women's colleges.

Many women were glad to see college courses broadened to meet their perceived needs as homemakers. However, this usually meant that women's post-college lives turned out to consist mainly of domestic work, when their children were small. Later, when the children had grown and left home, some women honed these skills to perfection, preparing gourmet meals, for example, to impress their family and friends. But other women began to question whether these were really the kind of educational opportunities they had needed after all. Somewhat surprisingly, despite the conservative mood of the 1950s and the lack of opportunities or encouragement for women, many did make their mark in a wide range of disciplines.

WRITERS AND POETS

Women writers of the era included Carson McCullers, author of works of fiction that dealt with loneliness and isolation in the American

> ❝
>
> **EMOTIONAL PAIN**
>
> *What is reality*
> *To this synthetic doll*
> *Who should smile, who should shift gears,*
> *Should spring the doors open in a wholesome disorder,*
> *And have no evidence of ruin or fears?*
> *But I would cry,*
> *Rooted into the wall that*
> *Was once my mother,*
> *If I could remember how*
> *And if I had the tears.*
>
> From "Self in 1958," by Anne Sexton

South. Mary McCarthy wrote witty novels that explored political and moral problems of the time. Notable female poets included Marianne Moore, who said poets should offer the reader "imaginary gardens with real toads in them." Her best-known poems feature animals and are written in a clear, precise language.

A number of female poets whose careers took off in the 1950s specialized in a "confessional" style of writing that offered the reader a view of their emotional anguish. The most famous among them, Anne Sexton and Sylvia Plath, both took their own lives while relatively young. Diane di Prima was an important figure in the Beat movement; in addition to writing poetry, she co-founded the New York Poets Theater and founded the Poets Press, which published the works of many new writers. In 1950, Gwendolyn Brooks became the first African American to win a Pulitzer Prize for poetry. Her poems in this period focused on poor black people living in cities. Brooks's

WOMEN OF COURAGE AND CONVICTION

MARGUERITE HIGGINS (1920–66)

Marguerite Higgins was a war correspondent during World War II and the Korean War, where she covered the fall of the capital Seoul to North Korean forces. When women reporters were banned from the front line, Higgins refused to leave and continued to file stories. She accompanied the marines when they landed in Inchon, 200 miles (320 kilometers) behind the North Korean lines, on September 15, 1950. Her personal style of reporting the war was popular with the American public. While covering the Vietnam War in 1954, she narrowly escaped stepping on the land mine that killed her colleague Robert Capa. She died of a tropical disease contracted in Vietnam.

Right: War correspondent Marguerite Higgins adjusts her helmet while typing up a news story from a battle zone in Germany in 1945.

novel of 1953, *Maud Martha*, was a portrait of a ghetto woman
who believes she is ugly but finally stands up for herself and defends
her dignity.

ARTISTS AND DESIGNERS
The art world reflected a fresh outlook following the end of World
War II with new styles emerging, most notably abstract expressionism.
Rooted in New York, this movement was founded by a generation

Below: Artist Elaine de Kooning
(1918–89) at work on a series
of portraits of President John F.
Kennedy in her studio in New York
City in the early 1960s.

Actress Marilyn Monroe (1926–62), the ultimate blond bombshell, lit up the movie screen but led a troubled life. Her talents were ruthlessly exploited by Hollywood, and she died tragically young.

of "rebel artists." Prolific women artists included Isabel Bishop, Elaine de Kooning, Marion Greenwood, Loren MacIver, and Irene Rice Pereira. De Kooning painted portraits as well as abstracts, Greenwood painted murals and was a war artist, MacIver painted landscapes and street scenes, and abstract painter Pereira was influenced by the Bauhaus, a German art and architecture movement. Modernist textile designer Anni Albers was also influenced by the Bauhaus movement. She was an expert weaver and created "pictorial weavings" based on ancient Peruvian and Mexican textiles.

MOVIE STARS AND FAIRY-TALE PRINCESSES

The 1950s was the decade of Technicolor movies and exaggerated sex symbols. During World War II and the Korean War, pinup girls such as Marilyn Monroe, Lana Turner, Rita Hayworth, and Betty Grable had inspired fighting men. But when war ended, the power of these actresses was no longer required to strengthen soldiers' nerves and they were transformed into harmless sex kittens. The movies showed them as women in need of protection, who, with a little male help, could be turned into devoted wives. An alternative blond bombshell of the 1950s was Grace Kelly. Her aristocratic "ice maiden" style was admired and copied by many women, who saw her marriage to Prince Rainer III of Monaco in 1956 as a fairy tale come true.

WOMEN BEHIND THE SCENES

In theater and the movies, women also made important contributions behind the scenes. In 1953, actress Julie Bovasso

TURNING POINT

MOVIE STAR INVENTOR

In 1942, beautiful Hollywood actress Hedy Lamarr took out a patent on her invention of a military communications system. She donated her idea to the war effort so that the Allies could transmit messages without being blocked or intercepted by the Nazis. Her spread spectrum technology is still the principle behind cell phones and much military defense technology.

founded the Tempo Theater Company in New York City and brought plays by European writers such as Jean Genet and Eugene Ionesco to the United States. In the late 1940s and early 1950s, the husband-and-wife writing team of Garson Kanin and Ruth Gordon scripted two witty movie vehicles for Spencer Tracy and Katharine Hepburn. The onscreen relationship of the two stars was believed to reflect Gordon and Kanin's offscreen marriage. Gordon was an actress as well as a writer and (unusually for the time) was sixteen years older than Kanin; the couple received Academy Award nominations for both screenplays. Costume designer Edith Head had a long career in Hollywood, but the 1950s were her heyday. Known for her no-nonsense working style, she designed wardrobes for most of the major stars, including Bette Davis, Elizabeth Taylor, Grace Kelly, Ingrid Bergman, and Kim Novak.

SCIENTISTS AND ENTREPRENEURS

In addition to Barbara McClintock, women scientists of the era included writer and marine biologist Rachel Carson, whose books on ocean life—*The Sea Around Us* and *The Edge of the Sea*—became unexpected bestsellers. She was one of the first people to draw attention to the fragility of the environment and, from 1945, warned about the use of the highly toxic DDT as a pesticide. In 1950, cosmetics manufacturer and entrepreneur Hazel Bishop invented the "kiss-proof" Lasting Lipstick, which left a stain on the lips that lasted hours ("It stays on you . . . not on him"). Between 1950 and 1953, Bishop's lipstick sales rose from $50,000 to $4.5 million, and by 1954, they exceeded $10 million a year.

Right: Scientist Rachel Carson (1907–64) drew attention to the influence people had on their environment and challenged the idea that nature existed to serve the needs of humans.

> ### CONSERVATION ISSUES
>
> *"The more clearly we can focus our attention on the wonders and realities of the universe about us, the less taste we shall have for destruction."*
>
> Rachel Carson, 1954

CHAPTER 7

THE NON-WHITE EXPERIENCE

IN THE 1940S AND 1950S, THE LIVES OF BLACK WOMEN were very different from those of most of their white contemporaries. Racism was prevalent in the United States, particularly in the South, where violence against black people, including lynching, was not uncommon. Elsewhere, segregated neighborhoods meant that middle-class suburbia tended to be off-limits for black people unless they were gardeners or domestic workers. Segregation by race extended to facilities and services such as housing, schools, restaurants, and transportation. Black people lived mainly in the poorer areas of cities, where they developed thriving subcultures rooted in historical traditions. During the 1950s, a significant number of Hispanic people also moved into urban areas.

TURNING POINT

STRANGE FRUIT

In 1938, Billie Holiday performed "Strange Fruit" for the first time at Café Society, an integrated nightclub in Greenwich Village, New York City. This song, about the horrors of lynching in the South, was based on a poem by Abel Meeropol, a Jewish schoolteacher from the Bronx. "Strange Fruit" would later become Holiday's best-selling record and an anthem for the civil rights movement.

"Southern trees bear strange fruit,

Blood on the leaves and blood at the root,

Black body swinging in the southern breeze,

Strange fruit hanging from the poplar trees."

Right: With her unique style of phrasing and tempo, vocalist Billie Holiday (1915–59) had a huge influence on jazz and pop singing.

LIVING CONDITIONS

In 1939, 92 percent of black people were living in poverty. Economic conditions had a profound effect on roles in the homes of blacks and poor whites. Widespread long-term unemployment meant that many men lacked self-respect and confidence; this led to women being forced to take on a dominant role in the family and to greater equality between partners. In these families, the person who earned the money held the power, and this was often the woman rather than the man of the house. In reality, the black matriarch was a low-paid worker or welfare recipient, but at home she and her husband were on a more equal footing than middle-class white couples. While many white women longed for more independence, the author Maya Angelou observed that many black women would have preferred a traditional role as a wife and mother with a well-paid husband.

WORK

In 1939, the average annual income for white women was $568, compared with $962 for white men; black women earned an average of $246. They did, however, benefit more than any other group of female workers from the increased mobility and work opportunities offered during World War II. Before the war, over 70 percent worked as domestic servants in private homes, while another 20 percent labored as

Above: A family of sharecroppers eke out a living on Bayou Bourbeau plantation in Louisiana. By 1940, the income of African-American working women was still less than half that of white women.

> ### THE OTHER SIDE OF THE FENCE
>
> *"[Too often we] found ourselves . . . unmarried, bearing lonely pregnancies and wishing for two and a half children each who would gurgle happily behind that picket fence while we drove our men to work in our friendly-looking station wagons."*
>
> Maya Angelou, from her autobiography *Singin' and Swingin' and Gettin' Merry Like Christmas*, 1977

Right: The war years saw a huge increase in the number of African-American men and women moving to urban areas for work.

IMPROVEMENTS IN EDUCATION

Psychologist and civil rights activist Mamie Phipps Clark carried out groundbreaking studies on race and child development. With her husband, Kenneth Bancroft Clark, she founded the Northside Center for Child Development in Harlem in 1946. Her work contributed to the ruling of the U.S. Supreme Court that determined that segregation in public education was unconstitutional.

agricultural workers in the fields. The call for new workers in the early 1940s caused many black women to leave their low-paid employment for better-paid jobs and improved conditions in the war industries. At last, black women found themselves working for a reasonable wage in a safe, clean environment. In some workplaces, African-American, Hispanic, and white women employees sat together for the first time.

DISCRIMINATION

The migration of large numbers of black people to northern and western cities in search of work led to an acute housing shortage. During the war years, the black population of Detroit doubled. In Baltimore, ten people were crowded into each house. People were crammed into racial ghettos, where overcrowding and poverty resulted in high maternal and infant mortality—twice that of whites.

After the war, more black women than white women were laid off from work. Many of them were eventually rehired, but at lower wages. Whereas white women tended to be employed in clerical jobs, black women made up a growing proportion of the industrial workforce. In 1941, President Roosevelt signed Executive Order 8802, which created the Fair Employment Practices Committee. This banned discrimination in the defense industries. Changes in the working lives of African-American women during this period gave them the confidence to fight for improvements to their lives and the ending of segregation.

STEREOTYPING

"Mammy" was a caricature of a black slave woman that dated from the 19th century. Whites used this stereotype to support their continuing oppression of African-American people and to sell products from postcards to detergent. Mammy was an overweight, cheery, loyal servant to a white family—seemingly content with her lot and ready to offer a shoulder to cry on in times of need. Highly talented black actresses were regularly typecast as mammies in movies during the 1930s, 1940s, and 1950s. Hattie McDaniel won an Academy Award for playing such a role in *Gone With the Wind* (1939). When criticized by black activists for repeatedly playing mammies, McDaniel responded: "Why should I complain about making seven thousand dollars a week playing a maid? If I didn't, I'd be making seven dollars a week actually being one."

Below: Hattie McDaniel (right) was a fine actress whose film roles included that of Mammy in *Gone With the Wind*, shown here. McDaniel was also a singer-songwriter, comedian, stage actress, and radio and TV performer.

WOMEN OF COURAGE AND CONVICTION

ALICE COACHMAN
(1923–)

At the 1948 Olympic Games in London, high jumper Alice Coachman became the first African-American woman to win an Olympic gold medal. Alice had fought against adversity to reach this point. As a child growing up in the segregated South, she trained herself to sprint on dirt roads and in fields because black children were not allowed to take part in organized athletic activities at school. She broke her high school and college high-jump records without wearing shoes. Although an injury to her back troubled her at the 1948 Olympic Games, she jumped 5 feet, 6.25 inches on her first try. After this victory, she retired from athletics but remained a supporter of new talent in the field. She later formed the Alice Coachman Track and Field Foundation, a nonprofit organization that provides assistance to young athletes and helps former Olympic athletes adjust to life afterward.

WOMEN OF COURAGE AND CONVICTION

ROSA PARKS
(1913–2005)

On December 1, 1955, in Montgomery, Alabama, a seamstress named Rosa Parks was arrested for refusing to obey the order of the driver of a bus she was riding to give up her seat to a white man. Her act of defiance was an inspiration to others and led to the Montgomery Bus Boycott, in which thousands of black people refused to ride the buses.

WOMEN IN THE CIVIL RIGHTS MOVEMENT

Gathering momentum in the 1940s, the civil rights movement lobbied and demonstrated for equal treatment of non-white citizens. Black women and girls took part in large numbers from the start, gaining personal strength and valuable experience from organizing marches and rallies. They joined unions and were instrumental in fighting for equal pay and working conditions.

Mary McLeod Bethune was the daughter of former slaves from South Carolina. She became a civil rights leader and set up a school for black students in Daytona Beach, Florida, which would later become Bethune-Cookman University. She was also an advisor to President Roosevelt and served as consultant to the U.S. Secretary of War for the selection of the first female officer candidates.

HISPANIC PECAN SHELLERS

Labor activist Luisa Moreno was a major figure in the struggle for Hispanic civil rights. In 1938, she was involved in a strike that broke out among pecan shellers in Texas. The industry was one of the lowest paid in the United States, with a typical wage ranging from

Below: A mural celebrates the achievements of labor activist and champion of Hispanic civil rights Luisa Moreno (1907–92).

$2 to $3 a week. On January 31, 1938, 12,000 San Antonio pecan shellers, mostly Hispanic women, walked out on their jobs when the managers announced a cut in their wages. A three-month strike followed. Eventually, the pecan shellers succeeded in getting around half of their wage cut restored.

Moreno sought to bring together all associations working for Hispanics, not only for Mexican Americans but also for Puerto Ricans, Cuban Americans, and others. In 1939, she played an important role in planning the National Congress of Spanish Speaking People. The meeting was held in Los Angeles and attracted labor union officials, community organizers, educators, and religious leaders.

INTO THE 1950S
During the 1940s, African-American women fought with some success to end discrimination in the meatpacking industry, where they were always assigned the dirtiest, least desirable jobs. Nevertheless, racism persisted into the 1950s in the pink- and white-collar sectors, where black women were usually given the more menial and less "visible" jobs—in housekeeping or in the kitchen.

During the struggle for civil rights in the mid-1950s, activist Ella Baker drew on her thirty years of experience to advise Martin Luther King Jr. A young woman named Autherine Lucy Foster was the first black student to sit in a University of Alabama classroom in February 1956. And in 1957, at Little Rock, Arkansas, nine black teenagers, six of whom were female, faced mob violence and physical and verbal abuse when they enrolled in a racially segregated high school.

PUBLIC SERVANTS
Examples of African-American women holding public office during this period were the exception rather than the rule. However, the hindrance was often their gender rather than their race. Shirley Chisholm, a black congresswoman

TURNING POINT

MARIAN ANDERSON CONCERT
On Easter Sunday, 1939, African-American singer Marian Anderson performed an open-air concert on the steps of the Lincoln Memorial in Washington, D.C. A conservative women's group called Daughters of the American Revolution had refused to give a black woman permission to sing in Constitution Hall. As a result, Anderson was forced to sing outside, but at least the concert went ahead.

Below: On April 9, 1939, Marian Anderson (1897–1993) gives an open-air recital on the steps of the Lincoln Memorial before a crowd of 75,000 people.

in the 1960s, stated: "I was constantly bombarded by both men and women that I should return to teaching, a woman's vocation, and leave politics up to the men."

Earlier in the century, the Roosevelt administration had seen some developments in this field, largely thanks to the intervention of Eleanor Roosevelt. In 1938, Crystal Fauset, the director of the Philadelphia office of the Works Progress Administration, was elected to the Pennsylvania House of Representatives. She was the first black woman to be elected to a major public office in the United States. In 1939, Jane Bolin became the first African-American female judge in the United States. And in 1950, Judge Edith Sampson was appointed as a delegate to the United Nations and to the North Atlantic Treaty Organization (NATO), where she was a strong advocate for the world's underprivileged children.

Above: Jane Bolin was the first African-American woman to graduate from Yale Law School and the first black woman judge in the United States. "Everyone else makes a fuss about it," she said in 1993, "but I didn't think about it, and I still don't."

GETTING OFF THE GROUND

"*Mama exhorted [told] her children at every opportunity to 'jump at de sun.' We might not land on the sun, but at least we would get off the ground.*"

Author Zora Neale Hurston

PERFORMING ARTISTS

African-American women were prominent in music and the arts during this era. Famous opera singers included sopranos Adele Addison, Muriel Rahn, and Mattiwilda Dobbs. Choreographer Katherine Dunham revolutionized American dance when she introduced African and Caribbean rhythms and movements to the form. The "Dunham technique" became a major influence in the careers of many performing artists. Margaret Bonds was one of the first black composers to gain recognition in the United States; she was also a classical pianist.

Musical theater performers included Dorothy Dandridge, who became the first black woman nominated for an Academy Award in the category of Best Actress for her performance in *Carmen Jones* in 1954; Pearl Bailey, who appeared in George Gershwin's *Porgy and Bess* in 1959; dancer, actress, and singer Carmen de Lavallade; and singer and movie star Lena Horne. Other artists included stage and screen actress Claudia McNeil, and Moms Mabley, who in 1939 made history by becoming the first comedian to play the famed Apollo Theater in Harlem. Elegant and intelligent actress Maidie Norman appeared in several movies throughout the 1950s, though the roles seldom did justice to her skills.

> ▶ **BREAKTHROUGH BIOGRAPHY**
>
> ### LORRAINE HANSBERRY (1930–65)
>
> Playwright and civil rights activist Lorraine Hansberry grew up in Chicago but moved to New York City at about age twenty to work on magazines such as the *Village Voice*. At age twenty-nine, she launched her play on Broadway, *A Raisin in the Sun*, about a black family trying to better its living conditions and gain self-respect. Hansberry was the first black playwright to receive the New York Drama Critics Circle award for the year's best play. She was active throughout the civil rights era and counted Robert Kennedy and Martin Luther King Jr. among her friends. Her life was tragically cut short by cancer at age thirty-four.

Left: Dorothy Dandridge (1922–65) was a beautiful actress and vocalist who worked her way up from nightclub singer to Hollywood star. Her career was brief, however, and her troubled life ended in an accidental drug overdose.

CHAPTER 8
THE PERIOD IN BRIEF

STARTING IN THE WAR YEARS AND CONTINUING INTO THE 1950S, women went out to work in growing numbers. By 1960, over ten million homes had both husband and wife at work—an increase of 333 percent from 1940. Moreover, the women going out to work, albeit part time, were mostly from those middle-class families who had supposedly found contentment in domesticity during the 1950s.

LOOKING FEAR IN THE FACE

"You gain strength, courage and confidence by every experience in which you really stop to look fear in the face. You are able to say to yourself, 'I have lived through this horror. I can take the next thing that comes along.' You must do the thing you think you cannot do."

Eleanor Roosevelt

IMPROVED WORKING CONDITIONS

During World War II, millions of women moved into jobs vacated by men. This shift gave them improved status and self-esteem and a first taste of financial independence. They found themselves doing challenging jobs they would never have dreamed of trying before, and they gained a sense of independence and empowerment that many of them would be

Below: Still going strong in 1960, Eleanor Roosevelt appears at a rally at the New York Coliseum in support of presidential candidate John F. Kennedy (left) and his running mate, Lyndon B. Johnson.

Right: A female technician does maintenance work on an early computer. As the 1950s gave way to the 1960s, women began to marry later and have fewer children, and more women went out to work.

unwilling to give up. During the 1940s and 1950s, non-white and working-class women workers joined labor unions to lobby for better pay and conditions. Through this, they discovered the power that comes from getting together to fight for a common cause. Women applied this sense of mutual supportiveness to their activities in the emerging civil rights movement.

JOB SATISFACTION

After the war, as servicemen returned home looking for jobs, women were encouraged to resume their traditional role as housewives and mothers. A boom in suburban building occurred as married couples moved out of the cities to commuter areas. The pressure on women to stay at home was intense. Soon, however, consumerism sparked the quest for a better standard of living, so women felt the need to seek paid employment again. Once more, many of them found that work gave them satisfaction, recognition, independence, and a sense of usefulness. It also gave them a greater say in the economic decisions of the family, and they enjoyed meeting other workers and gained social skills and confidence.

Once women had left their conventional roles as housewives for jobs outside the home, they did not go back. They were creating a new and permanent sphere for themselves in the workplace. Women's progress was not halted in the 1950s, as is generally believed, even though most women did low-paid work that was subordinate to men. The progress women made in the 1950s in establishing themselves as a presence in the labor force, the arts and sciences, and in administration laid the groundwork for the drive for equality in the 1960s.

OFF TO WORK

"The slick magazine idea of the American woman in her negligee kissing her husband goodbye as he goes off to work and she returns to her kitchen full of machines to do the work for her is hardly a true one . . . she is off to work too. She has climbed over the walls of her kitchen, has worked in the market place, and learned about the world beyond the doormat."

Women's advocate Esther Peterson, "Woman at Work in the United States," c. 1955

Timeline

1938   Crystal Bird Fauset is the first black woman elected to a state legislature. The Fair Labor Standards Act establishes minimum wages and maximum hours for both sexes and forbids employment of children under age sixteen.

1939   Russian, Jewish, and Chinese women at a Los Angeles cannery walk out for higher pay, improved working conditions, and union recognition. After winning the national 100-meter freestyle championship, swimmer Esther Williams establishes a career as a movie star.

1940   One-fifth of white women and one-third of black women are wage earners.

1941   The United States enters World War II. Some 350,000 women serve.

1942   The Planned Parenthood Federation of America is established.

1943   The All-American Girl's Softball (later Baseball) League is founded.

1944   Viola White is arrested on a bus in Montgomery, Alabama, for violating segregation laws.

1945   The end of World War II sees women workers lose their jobs to returning servicemen. The United Nations is created. Eleanor Roosevelt is named the U.S. delegate and becomes chairperson of the Committee on Human Rights.

1946   Eudora Welty publishes *Delta Wedding*, her first full-length novel. *North and South* is the first volume of poetry by Elizabeth Bishop. In 1950, an expanded version, together with *A Cold Spring*, wins a Pulitzer Prize. Ruth Ann Koesun is the first Asian-American soloist and principal dancer with a national company, the American Ballet Theater.

1947   350,000 telephone workers, two-thirds of whom are women, go on strike against American Telephone and Telegraph. An influential anti-feminist book, *The Modern Woman: The Lost Sex*, is co-written by Marynia Farnham.

1948   The Women's Armed Services Integration Act gives women permanent status in the armed forces. Alice Coachman is the first black woman to win an Olympic gold medal, in the high jump.

1949   Actress Stella Adler founds the Stella Adler Conservatory of Acting in New York City. Babe Didrikson wins the U.S. Women's Open for the third year running.

1950   The United States enters the Korean War. Large numbers of women, nurses, and WACs are stationed in Japan. Over 120,000 servicewomen serve stateside. Senator Margaret Chase Smith delivers her "Declaration of Conscience" speech, denouncing the extremism of Joseph McCarthy.

1951	Janet Collins becomes the first African-American prima ballerina of the New York Metropolitan Opera. Marion Donovan invents and manufactures disposable diapers; she later sells her company for $1 million.
1952	Soprano Dorothy Maynor is the first black singer allowed to perform at the Daughters of the American Revolution's Constitution Hall in Washington, D.C.
1953	Jacqueline Cochran is the first woman to pilot a plane faster than the speed of sound. Playwright and former member of Congress Clare Boothe Luce is appointed ambassador to Italy. Oveta Culp Hobby, director of the Women's Auxiliary Army Corps (WAAC) during World War II, is the first Secretary of Health, Education, and Welfare.
1954	Katherine Dexter McCormick finances the first experimental trials of oral contraceptives on humans. Dorothy Dandridge is the first African American to be nominated for an Academy Award as best actress in the musical *Carmen Jones*.
1955	Rosa Parks triggers the Montgomery, Alabama, bus boycott by refusing to give up her seat to a white person. Women earn an average of 63 cents for every dollar earned by men. The figure drops over the next decade.
1956	Autherine Lucy, a black student, is admitted to the University of Alabama. When she arrives, she is met with rioting. She is expelled for criticizing the university's lack of support during the incident.

The number of women in the workforce reaches nearly thirteen million, up from 8.5 million in 1947.

1957	In Little Rock, Arkansas, U.S. soldiers escort nine black students, led by civil rights activist Daisy Bates, to school after the Arkansas National Guard has been called to keep them out. African-American tennis player Althea Gibson wins both the singles and doubles (with Darlene Hard) titles at Wimbledon, as well as the U.S. Open.
1958	Ella Fitzgerald wins the first two Grammy Awards for female vocalist.
1959	Lorraine Hansberry's *A Raisin in the Sun*, the first play by a black woman to be staged on Broadway, wins the New York Drama Critics' Circle Award. *A Century of Higher Education for Women*, by Mabel Newcomer, reports that the proportion of women college students has dropped from 47 percent in 1920 to 35.2 percent in 1958.
1960	The Food and Drug Administration (FDA) approves the first oral contraceptive, fostering a sexual revolution and making family planning possible for women. Women now earn only 60 cents for every dollar earned by men—a decline since 1955. Women of color earn only 42 cents. Harper Lee's *To Kill a Mocking Bird*, a novel about southern bigotry, becomes a bestseller and wins a Pulitzer Prize the following year.

Glossary and Further Information

abstract expressionism A school of painting that flourished in the United States from the late 1940s to the early 1960s. It was characterized by its lack of representation and its freedom of emotional expression and technique.

adultery Sexual intercourse by a married person with someone to whom she or he is not married.

amendment An article added to the Constitution.

auxiliary A person or role that gives additional help or support.

aviatrix A female pilot.

Beat movement Young people in the 1950s and early 1960s, who wrote and were interested in poetry, novels, and modern jazz. They valued self-expression and rejected conventional society.

chromosome A structure found in living cells that carries genetic information in the form of genes.

civil rights movement A movement led by African Americans from the 1940s to the 1980s that fought for equal social and political rights. Protests took the form of marches, non-violent demonstrations, boycotts, and sit-ins.

communism A way of organizing a country so that all the land and industry belong to the state and all the profits are shared among the people.

contraceptive A device or drug that prevents pregnancy.

cryptologist A person who studies codes.

DDT Dichlorodiphenyltrichloroethane, a toxic insecticide now banned in many countries.

economic Relating to the economy—the wealth of a country, especially in terms of the production and consumption of goods and services.

entrepreneur A person who takes the risk of setting up a business, hoping to make a profit.

federal A system of government in which a country is divided into states, which form a union but which have independent control of their own internal affairs.

feminism Support for women's rights on the grounds of equality between the sexes.

genetic engineering The selection and manipulation of genes to create desirable characteristics.

genome The entire sequence of DNA in an individual species.

ghetto An area of a city, usually poor, occupied by a minority group.

icon A person who is widely admired and who symbolizes a movement or era.

induce To speed up the process of childbirth through the use of drugs.

labor union A group of workers who have organized to gain fair working conditions or pay.

lobbied Attempted to pressure or influence.

lynching The killing of a person without trial, usually by hanging.

matriarch A powerful woman who is head of a family.

menial Unskilled and of low status.

migration A move from one area to another.

North Atlantic Treaty Organization (NATO) A military alliance of North American and European countries, founded in 1949, for the defense of Europe against the perceived Soviet threat.

patriotic Vigorously supporting one's country.

pharmacologist A scientist who specializes in the uses, effects and action of drugs.

progesterone A hormone.

prohibit Forbid.

propaganda Information, often distorted, intended to promote a cause or persuade people to do something.

psychologist A person whose job it is to study the human mind and its functions, especially in terms of behavior.

psychotherapy The treatment of mental illness by psychological means rather than by using drugs or surgery.

quilling A type of decorative craftwork.

quota The number of students allowed into a college each year.

segregation Describes a situation in which different ethnic groups live in separate areas.

sharecropper A tenant farmer who gives part of his or her crop as rent.

simulating Imitating.

sociologist A person who studies how society is structured and how it functions.

strafing Attacking a target with machine-gun fire from a low-flying aircraft.

strike When workers refuse to work as a protest.

subculture A cultural group within a larger culture, often having interests or beliefs particular to that smaller group.

suffragist A person who believes in equal voting rights, especially for women.

taboo Forbidden.

transposon A strand of DNA that can be moved from one part of a genome to another part, or from one genome to another.

BOOKS

Nonfiction

Gourley, Catherine. *Gidgets and Women Warriors: Perceptions of Women in the 1950s and 1960s* (*Images and Issues of Women in the Twentieth Century*). Minneapolis, Minnesota: Twenty-First Century Books, 2007.

Gourley, Catherine. *Rosie and Mrs. America: Perceptions of Women in the 1930s and 1940s* (*Images and Issues of Women in the Twentieth Century*). Minneapolis, Minnesota: Twenty-First Century Books, 2007.

Gourley, Catherine. *War, Women, and the News: How Female Journalists Won the Battle to Cover World War II*. New York: Atheneum, 2007.

Keller, Emily. *Frances Perkins: First Woman Cabinet Minister* (20th Century Leaders). Greensboro, North Carolina: Morgan Reynolds Publishing, 2006.

May, Elaine Tyler. *Pushing the Limits: American Women 1940–1961*. Oxford, UK: Oxford University Press, 1998.

Nathan, Amy. *Yankee Doodle Gals: Women Pilots of World War II*. Des Moines, Iowa: National Geographic Children's Books, 2001.

Price, Sean. *Rosie the Riveter: Women in World War II* (*History Through Primary Sources*). Milwaukee, Wisconsin: Raintree, 2008.

Fiction

Lee, Harper. *To Kill a Mocking Bird*. 1960. Fiftieth Anniversary edition: New York: HarperCollins, 2010.

Welty, Eudora. *Delta Wedding*. 1946. Boston, Massachusetts: Houghton Mifflen Harcourt, 1991.

WEB SITES

http://www.kclibrary.lonestar.edu

http://www.pbs.org/wgbh/americanexperience/u

http://www.teacheroz.com/WWIIHomefront.htm

INDEX